MADAME SASOO GOES BATHING

Madame Sasoo Goes Bathing

TIM LIARDET

Shoestring Press

ISBN 978-1-907356-64-3

Cover image: Pape Moe (Mysterious Water) 1893–1894,
Paul Gauguin, © Art Institute of Chicago 2013

Designed and typeset by Gerry Cambridge
gerry.cambridge@btinternet.com
Set in Adobe Garamond Pro

Printed by Clydeside Press, 37 High Street, Glasgow G1 1LX
clydesidepress@btconnect.com

Published by Shoestring Press
19, Devonshire Avenue, Beeston, Nottinghamshire, NG9 1BS
(0115) 925 1827
www.shoestringpress.co.uk

CONTENTS

ACKNOWLEDGEMENTS

Acknowledgements are due to the editors of the following journals and newspapers in which some of these poems first appeared, or will appear: *Agenda*, *Ars Interpres* (Stockholm), *Birmingham Poetry Review* (USA), *The Guardian*, *The London Magazine*, *Long Poem Magazine*, *The Manhattan Review*, *Poetry Ireland Review*, *Poetry London*, *Poetry Review*, *New Writing 12*.

'Madame Sasoo Goes Bathing' first appeared in *New Writing 12* (ed. Morrison, Rogers and Adebayo, Picador/British Council), and was reprinted in *The Guardian*. 'Darwin in Mauritius'—which first appeared in *The London Magazine*—is loosely based upon a short extract from Darwin's *Voyage of the Beagle*, 1839. Darwin reached Mauritius on 29th April 1836. He wrote 'The elephant is the only one at present on the island; but it is said others will be sent for'. 'At Gris-Gris'—which first appeared in its entirety in *Long Poem Magazine*—is indebted to countless articles and websites which examine the strange mutations of climate change. A debt of gratitude is owed to Richard Kerridge for invaluable ecocritical overview; to Fiona Sampson for bringing to the manuscript her editorial acuity. And to Miranda Liardet, but for whom.

for Miranda

In the eighth of June, during the night, after a sixty-three days' voyage, sixty-three days of feverish expectancy, we perceived strange fires, moving in zig-zags on the sea. From the sombre sky a black cone with jagged indentions became disengaged...It was the summit of a mountain submerged at the time of one of the great deluges. Only the very point rose above the waters. A family fled thither and founded a new race—and then the corals climbed up along it, surrounding the peak, and in the course of the centuries builded a new land.

—*Noa Noa: The Tahiti Journals of Paul Gauguin*, 1894, Paul Gauguin

THE INTRICATE FEATURES OF MONSTERS

The wood-wasp thumps, thumps between window and blind.
When I cautiously pull back the blind—*Sweet Jesus*.
I could live with the mic into which it moaned and made
a noise less like the revs of a falsetto Suzuki
than the growl of an old English motorbike—
but not with the terrible, ten times enlarging, zoom.

THE BAMBOO TALKING BAMBOO-TALK

Ohhr—eeear, it sings, *aneeek, aneek, eeear*;
the trebles succumb to the bass-line of *eeeeeeaaaaaaarrr*.
These the receptors of the giant Chinese bamboo
receiving the purest hallowing note from Mars,
distilled through my cell-phone's mics into talk.
This the chatter of all its stems talking at once,
the shiver of one note passing through them,
all stems in that moment heckling each other,
all stems, all at once, outshouting each other.
This the racket of the wind harassing its flutes
like an outbreak of imbeciles laughing.

Aneeeeeek, arah-arah—neeep, neeep, neeep, neeep,
says the bamboo, as if everything is loose—
now old squeeze-box, now rodent in trap,
now the high-pitched wailing of the dead.
Step into the note-shiver, it says, then step through it
before it goes out of human hearing.
For every presumptuous step you take
imagine a blinder, ten metre stride.
Imagine my knuckles, it says, now gigantic.
I'm Brobdingnagian grasses, magnified.
Neeeeep, neeeeep, it sings, *neeeeep, neeeeep, neeeeep*.

A MAN SEEKING EXPERIENCE ENQUIRES THE WAY OF THE WOMAN IN THE PAMPLEMOUSSES GARDEN

I watch you at a distance, my lovely apparatchik
by now flushed so hot and slightly flat-footed
in knee-length shorts, French plait, white baseball cap—
your old Praktika swings one way, shoulder to hip,
your back-pack pharmacy the other. You prop an arm
and trail the other idly through the gloom
of giant figs that have grown to a hundred feet,
and from buckled roots grown remarkably straight:
standing there composed, while I hunker in the dirt,
you teach me (because I need to learn) the art
of wanting without reserve to be part of this
green and boiling amplitude which is
guarded by tall, white gates. Inside it, you grow hot,
swig water, in the steepling Celsius sweat,
and among the tree-boles never relinquish
that *poise*. For my part, I crouch to one side and wish
first to catch a little of the lotus leaf's
humped arts of repelling moisture—the brief-
est spillage of moisture like mercury, shot
from the surface at first touch, whose lot
is to cling awhile for all its life to the skin
of its apparently ungracious tropical heroine,
be steam, then nothing. Your thoughts absorb the wet—
they drink, they open up and are beset
by the soft excitements around you, while mine
tremble, slide and are repelled, can only hold on
as well as the droplet of sweat that eschews
my nose and my chin, and drips on my shoes.

AT GRIS-GRIS

'...a great perturbation in nature'
Macbeth

I

What I saw, or thought I saw through binoculars,
at first seemed like a man, three hundred metres out

from the sluggish heat and palms of Gris-Gris,
emerging from waves, then sinking beneath them

as if, were it a man, he was learning how to drown.
As the mass moved nearer, as the glasses found it again,

it was clearly not a man but a beast the like of which
had never been seen in these waters, floundering

and blundering into the shallows where, though
rocked by waves, it showed itself—that mouth

thrown open in a sort of hoarse, toothless cry
from among its deep shawls of blubber as it reared up

and seemed to sprawl larger and larger
before beginning to dissolve from the water's surface up,

all of it that was visible, began to disappear…
then there was only half, then less than half

left to dissolve in mid air, a monstrous torso and head
dissolving bone by bone, atom by atom. Gone.

2

Let me start again—stone and water. Water and fire,
fire and ice. This the sound of fire underwater where tall waves

collapse at Gris-Gris, the fire frothing white in them
whitening the whole coast like a fall of snow

and storming, storming against the black rocks—
the Indian Ocean, all of it, storming the rocks.

The latest wave collapses, then another, and the undertow
sets a million stones stumbling and fumbling

in delirium, strained by the force of the suck.
Above them the sand is glazed flawless, pulverised

by forty Celsius at the southernmost rock-pile
of this African island, pounded alike by heat and wave—

and wave after wave is duly sacrificed,
slapped down, hissing in to glaze smooth the incline

of pulverised sand over which it lunges
and as quickly steams off. Next land after this, Antarctica.

Next land after this—forty, four hundred
or four thousand miles south—Antarctica.

3

I have heard the waves talk, their sea-stone gossip,
not only of beasts but of icebergs. Once faceted

in drama like raw jade, they melt, grow toothless.
Four hundred square miles of Ice Shelf,

broken off, move slowly north… All's strange to itself.
Part wolf, part Sea-cow, part everything extinct,

part Antarctica's lugubrious stray,
the beast sighted at Gris-Gris, whatever it is, shows up

in waters warm enough to keep the Bludger-fish;
the Bludger-fish in waters cold enough to keep the beast.

There are mozzies in the belly of the penguin;
in the belly of the mozzies penguin blood.

The egg balanced on that foot, protectively,
contains God-knows-what… If there's a hex,

or a strangeness, the waves return them to Gris-Gris;
the hex is red earth, green palm and the blue,

the spell in the heat and the black rocks
mysteriously cast back over the waves.

4

When the beast was hauled ashore at Gris-Gris
the winch groaned, its long arm stuttered. The body weighed

two tons, I guessed, it bellyflopped on the sand,
outweighing all five men who had it rigged

in a bodice of chains. Stretched before it moved an inch,
first it wouldn't budge—stalled—then reluctantly budged:

when finally dragged, it flopped over brazenly to expose
the immensity of its belly, its thick grouty hide

so scratched and pitted and scarred—that Stone age snout.
Whatever it was, it was old, eighteen feet long if an inch

and, we agreed, blubbered for Forty-Below—
we thought it might be a drowned angel, nature's answer

to hypothermia destroyed by hypothermia.
Where the mouth hung open its molars gaped

in dumb remonstrance. The driver hit the gas
and the tractor snorted diesel-smoke, dragged it up the beach

while children sat astride, waving arms. It ploughed a trench
through wet sand which steamed into the heat.

5

I'd heard of hybrids, a beast part seal, part elephant,
a beast three quarters this, three quarters that,

but the day the beast was sighted at Gris-Gris
we'd no idea of what might have mated with what,

and dragged out the boat, took ropes, took tackle.
We took strength, threw the hull into breakers

that threw it back at us again and again.
Launched, it tipped and bucked—we climbed aboard,

all four of us, and rowed out over the waves
that reared and smashed against the prow. So convinced

of its physical mass, we imagined raising the beast
which at a distance had seemed to outgrow its strength

and founder like an island, sunk by its own weight...
We rowed and were lifted. This the spot, we said,

where it vanished into air and even as we spoke
realized that the beast was everywhere, all

around us, as if a freak snowstorm fell only
on the boat, and we had passed straight through it.

6

They were not binoculars after all but gun barrels,
and this a man so fearful of the creature's helplessness

when it dragged itself ashore at Gris-Gris, belly to gravel—
disturbed by so immense a beast's squeaky docility

he lifted both barrels of his old Martini-Medford rifle
he lifted both barrels of his old Martini-Medford rifle

and blasted straight through the cranium. The head
when the steel of the muzzle rested there on it

was blasted in two, the nostril-flaps sent flying
and bits of organic shrapnel blown in all directions

as if this were the meticulous sieving of fish-food
that fell with pitter-patter, plip-plop, in the breakers;

the snout and cranium were a burst blood-flower
steaming and smoking, steaming and smoking

and, like another sort of flower, the tongue a flame
ignited by rifle-heat, a flame that prospered awhile

in the mouth-space, turned yellow, orange,
turned blue, before like a firework it guttered out.

7

Flash memory, earbud and subwoofer, wheels in the sky
that spin to adjust the lens, he dreams, then slip

as if imperceptibly into reverse to halt
the satellite's rotation. The hatch opens on clouds

which slide apart like the hatch—through them, you can trace
the beast's heartbreaking journey, dreamt as it is

by the witchdoctor who turned a hundred twenty years ago
in the heat of Gris-Gris, praying to himself... Betrayed

by a spirit-heat shaped as island, he dreams, the beast
must drink the world's sins and be locked in a loop

of assassination—this the immense drum-thumping
of its ten kilo heart shrinking and expanding until

it must surely burst on its stalks, but does not.
Shot, the beast must arrive, be shot, arrive, be shot...

All he has, the witchdoctor sings in dream-song,
are trinkets, pouches, albino-teeth and fingernails

to charm away your terrifying visions
perpetually beamed from the sky, ungainly God.

THE SEGA DANCERS AS PRE-SEXUAL BEINGS

Their quims could be the point, finely dusted in hair,
but it's not their quims they shimmy to the drums;
it isn't their quims they trade here so much as their wings.
The Muslims stay away, from this profane slave-dance,
from these girls in their effrontery of energy.
But their quims are not the point so much as their wide wings
which are the metres of yellow they fly
and which leave a yellow halo on air to show us the dance
as well as the trailed ghost of it, to show us
in a vague mirror the flash of their backs
at the very moment they show us their fronts
at the moment they show us the tips of their wings.

They show their bellies like a butterfly
but it's not their quims they dance so much as their wings held out
to show us the crimson and the halo of crimson,
the dance and the ghost of the dance.
And when they flap their skirts so very wide indeed
each quim, finely dusted in hair, is the thing below
with which they do not quite know what to do
where the puberty-spider crouches, on the pubic bone,
and threatens to draw up their wings like a web in reverse.
They do not last for long, these creatures
that flap and flap and flap,
that swirl and buckle and soar
until the death of drum-beat like terrible rain,
(or the spider itself
deciding to move at last)
stops them;
and the verandah fly-trap burns up.

THE FLAME TREES OF TROU AUX BICHES

Not wishing for a moment to be upstaged
by clouds of blowsy blossom that cannot stay
although they are the queens of death and sex,
although it's light that holds them in its net:

not wishing to be thought at all plain
on their highway diet of two-stroke and gasoline;
not wishing to be outshone or overlooked
by the brilliant and branch-outreaching, swept

by salt-wind toward the inland spaces, they—
as if many gases leaked away
then rose and then spread thinly out
like tresses, like coiffures of cloud

that hung on the air—
set light to their hair.

DARWIN IN MAURITIUS

Of all the mysteries the elephant, he said—
on whose back he took a strolling seasick ride
south to examine rocks of elevated coral,
thrown gently from side to side, as light peppered
through the weft of his floppy brim under which
his prune-face lost itself in beard and thought.
Just the straps creaking, creaking against
the creaks of the bamboo through which they strolled:
how was it a beast, he thought, ten thousand pounds in weight
with inch-thick skin much given to insect bites—
drinking each day some forty gallons through
the sixty thousand muscles of which the length
of its languid and free-swinging trunk was made up—
could freight him with so soft, so noiseless a step.

MADAME SASOO GOES BATHING

Mme Sasoo, sombre, but determined
to overcome her nibbling inhibitions
and have the warm Indian Ocean lick
at will about her body, does not undress, but dresses up

from ankle to neck in brightly figured rayon
and wears her manly shoes to wade
from shore of drums into the tilt of water
with elbows aloft, all her attention below:

she is not young, but bears herself
with subtle dignity, though her costume clings, grows fat,
as the weight of water starts to rock
against her, and bullies her from left

to right, so she is like a high wire walker
riding out the admonishments
of the deluge, with grim composure,
holding that perfect crimson mark

in the middle of her forehead level
over the waves. At which stage, her doubts
regroup and call her back to the shore
where her towels, and Seiko, are safe

but every article of her nakedness
she wished the water could explore
and taste like expert tongues has been
stolen long before she dared to wade.

THE CROWDING

Displayed to us for the first time
in her yellow hijab, her brightly figured rayon,
her brooch and hijab-pin, her tiny gold-toed sandals,
her many-bangled wrist and henna'd hands,
her head didn't quite reach his shoulder—

here she is, he said to the summoned family,
my bride-to-be, your step-mother-to-be,
your step-grandmother, your step-sister, step-aunt,
your step-mother-in-law, your sister-in-law... Oh,
everyone got the physics of it—
                                the new mother
who had to be fitted into the English family;
the English family fitted into the new mother.

She stood there so tiny in a puddle of spilt light.

STEP

Stepmother, you give me the Qu'ran, you say
take care this is a holy book, we like to keep it wrapped
so, please, do not put it in the company of books
which are not as holy, please keep it in a place,
you say, that curtains it from worldly grime.
Your glance catches hold of my guilt
and the guilt of an indolent sinner, we know,
is the waste between us we must till…
I accept the book with gratitude, I know that of all books
at this date and time and latitude this
is the most important, and unwrap it
with such self-conscious dread I might bring
the fingers and thumbs of worldly grime
to its never-yet-broken pages, I bring
the fingers, the thumbs and the grime.
Your conviction so strong, I imagine you pick up
each of my fingers one by one
to inspect the state of the fingernail.
You flip over both palms, you hold them out
and bend them upward by the fingertips…
Yes, yes, before I open your book
I'll wash my hands again and again
in wool-fat, tea-tree, camomile, bergamot and kelp,
I'll stack each of these on a tray of hearts
as if binning the last more quickly to get to the next
and producing such excess of lather
might prove to indolent sinners everywhere
the many limitations of a bar of soap.

THE MAD AUNT'S VOICEMAIL

The black-eyed beans are bubbling…I thought
I'd ask…are you *there*, are you *there*? Are you *there*…?
if you'd any inkling whether your father's been
crushed, in this tunnel in Mecca? I know he's out

among the crowds… *Grief*, how those people are inclined
to mill—alarming pictures. Oh my dear, *poor John*;
is it true, *he's converted?* At the wedding, do you recall,
he read to us *there'll be couches encrusted with gold…*

or was it *with precious stones?* Well, I guess he'll have
no choice but lie on them. Clothed, one hopes.
Of course he's not a Muslim, John? And all
I was thinking—oh my dear—*remember?*—after

the Schubert impromptus I thundered out
of the old jalopy, he sounded so, so…*Oh*, if
he *has* been crushed we ought to know, you know…
that little cloudy wife of his is sweet but tiny

and all wrapped up in her brilliant shawls
perhaps bigger than she seems… in the snap he sent
she seems so, so…*Oh*, it'd be good to know
what you know, you know. *Hullo? Hullo? Hullo?*

OUD

Over the balcony rail she ditches
her eldest daughter's clothes into the street:
her fury hardly seems to know what
her many flailing hands do— *Non! Non! Non,*

she wails in squat Creole—*Fille perdue!*
Do not bring this non-Muslim man a step
nearer to the house is what she means. Over the rail go
the bottles of henna, oil and Oud

that drop like smell-bombs, until they overtake
the two metre sail of her chunni
somersaulting with a sort of weightless grace.
Descending even slower, dipping and rolling

the expanse of her jonquil saree
flapping very slowly if it flaps at all…
Down in the street, the bottle of Oud explodes
in a cataclysm of bits and vapours;

it flings odours everywhere, which breed odours;
a whiff of gaharu, a hint of jinko,
a trace of rose, jojoba, some cinnamon,
ylang-ylang, saffron, aloeswood…

THE BLINDING

That wallpaper—crazily hard on the eye
as a maker of migraines, but also a step
inside the beehive of superstition.
Rings. Rings. Rings. Rings that might have been left

in a row by a Chianti bottle's blood-cork
all around the room but you, Stepmother,
in humming panic set my hair-alarms
flailing like sensors. You said the rings were *eyes*—

you dreamt the whole room was riddled
by some terminal shoot-out, the shots
puncturing your Muslim probity as much
as the wallpaper and walls, like eye-beams.

So you cut patch after sticky-backed patch
and blacked out each in a pogrom of blinding,
a patch for each eye, to stopper the room,
as if you were trying to keep something in,

or out. I never went in, for fear every eye
might burn through its eye-patch and through me.
The swarm that broke in the room,
that broke suddenly, filled it with red light.

ARCIMBOLDO'S BULLDOG

You and I feared the dark was in the dog.
Kick it out howling, you howled. I kicked it out
but it crept back in, ears down. The dog,
you said, doesn't seem very pleased to see you.

Its deep sigh, I replied, suggests it's not
pleased to see you either. It might want to lick
a face, I said. (We watch, don't comment,
as it stoops to its hind-legs, which are agape).

The steam on its breath, you said, bespoils a home
for Muslim prayer. Kick it out, squealing.
It drips, I said, saliva on my boot...
Stepmother, though stray cats keep us apart,

these are the creaturely scraps of emotion,
the gobbets and slivers out of which
we glued the dog together, and once assembled
it befriended us, became mouthpiece and earpiece

through which we strained to hear but nonetheless
found a certain way to talk. The feedback *itched*,
itched in its ears. The dog was inclined
to grin more widely the deeper it scratched.

MÉMÉ

Being old, half blind, unable to read
or to write—deaf to all but the wheedling
whisper of her own reproachful voice—
for her talk was outer, a congestion of vowels

squabbling on her lips, the censorship
which rested like endurance on her mouth.
She had to be told we'd come all the way
from England, the awkward relations

who'd lately stalked the outer limits
of her imagination, who now stooped smiling
out of window-sun... There was the need to go
deeper, we knew, to step from slewed light,

there was the wariness of protocol.
Should we take hold of her hand limply,
take it and speak to her a few words
or stoop further toward the derelict place

of her cloth-folds, inertia and age;
should we tackle the thousand mile threshold
of taboo and of faith and of politics,
like dry mud between lip and cheek, to *kiss?*

LIFECYCLE OF COLOUR

after Gauguin

The strange machines of the vegetation
are sprayed in the moon's fish-belly white—
your island's leaf-coils exhausted by heat
were coated in this primer, patient for crimson
to absorb all colours but crimson,
green all colours but green, yellow all colours but yellow.

Colour's a creature of one day, you knew,
it crumbles through your fingers like dust, it forms
in the whizzing-fizzing particles of light,
a jitterbug in the photons and electrons
to which we say *yellow! crimson! green!* before they're consigned
to the job-lot—the gesso—of fish-belly white.

GIANT LILIES

Our sense of balance keeps us upright
while we stoop to our reflections out of the light,
out of space and clouds, over the lily pond's edge:
we watch a wide and evil mouth steer its head
down into the dark, slip out of sight,
as if its cellar were our lily-cratered state.
The water can no more make its monsters wet
than the stone it cannot penetrate.

The water stands in place—a block of scum;
as if the slimy glass of an old aquarium's
been withdrawn like a mould. Filtering crud,
the lily pads suck at a ceiling of mud.
Those coins have been lobbed, attempting to
rouse the lilies like crocodiles snoozing through
the pitter-patter, their jaws clamped shut.
Our flipped coin, trying to spin down, spins up.

Madame Sasoo Goes Bathing

IS PUBLISHED IN AN EDITION OF 150 COPIES
ON THE 28TH OF FEBRUARY, 2013,
OF WHICH THE FIRST 26 COPIES
ARE SIGNED AND LETTERED
ON THE COLOPHON
BY THE AUTHOR